LIGHT WITHOUT SHADOW

Man's Spiritual Pathway

by

Salvatore N. Balletto

Spirit is about the universe...so are you

The quotation on the following page, together with those on pages 31, and 51 were taken from a Buddhist retreat on Oahu, Hawaii. They were each carved into flat standing stones which were distributed along a winding path through a small tropical valley.

Copyright © 1992, by Savatore N. Balletto
Second Edition, Copyright © 2011
Thrid Edition, Copyright © 2017

All rights reserved. No part of this book may be reproduced or transmitted in any form or by any means, electronic or mechanical, including photocopying, recording, or by an information storage and retrieval system, without written permission of the author except where permitted by law.

*"Walk with knowing
or do not walk at all."*

PROLOGUE

*Word knowledge
is only the shadow of the truth.*

*It is not the truth
which only smiles in its drowsiness
as you attempt to
describe it, explain it, deny it, or prove it.*

The truth will awaken when you do!

The experience of the big water calls to you through the winds of your life. Do not fear the mountains and valleys. For through their pathways you will stand on the summit with only the sun on your back, the earth at your feet, and triumph in your hands.

Light Hawk

THE CONTINUUM

Prologue

This paper on man's spiritual pathway was part of a book I had written in a previous lifetime. I was a member of a religious sect in France. I was a monk in a monastery of a group that had a mixture of Christian and Buddhist philosophies. After my death the book was destroyed because it was deemed inappropriate. These excerpts were returned to me by Tao Chin Lao Sai E'.

Introduction

The pathway of Mankind is uniquely his own. He walks this pathway alone yet with all other men. There truly is no stepping back but progress for each to each is his own. The Continuum had no beginning and will have no end. It is infinitely dimensional yet uniquely individual. The Continuum knows no limits creates no force casts no shadow and exists for only one purpose to provide a pathway without end. The Continuum is complete, necessary, sufficient, and constant.

The Continuum knows no limits because it encompasses not only this physical plane but every physical plane where there is intelligent life form. In other words it entails and engages the entire universe. The Continuum knows no force because the spiritual laws (noninterference, avoidance of excess, and no distractions) apply to it. It casts no shadow because it is the purist form of self truth that exists in the universe.

The Continuum is complete in every dimension. Each facet fulfills itself perfectly. The completeness is natural without boundaries or void to achieve a purpose without end. To each for each without beginning without end. Your choices your karma the results will eternally be your name. Life calls to you. You can participate only thru the experience of its ever changing flow. You can bring about harmony, discord, walk, or run but you are Life's purpose for only one end.

The continuum is necessary for perfection given is not perfect at all. A lesson is learned only after it is experienced for experience given is not experience at all. You cannot escape the rapids, the waterfalls, the quiet places of life. But they can occur in your time and on your time. Lessons learned are necessary to reach your goal. Only thru the Continuum can you come closer to that end. The Continuum reaches for you with the opportunity to be the participant without end. Your place will emerge unique as you walk life's pathways of joy, sorrow, love, hatred, accomplishment, and delinquency. These and many more cannot escape your name. The necessity of the Continuum will complete your name for only one end.

The sufficiency is apparent. All is as one. One is as all. There is no force yet all progress cast in the light of self truth. There is no leader yet all walk to the same goal. Your choices create your pathway. Your pathway can be direct or indirect, smooth or rough, connected or disconnected, long or short, but never without purpose. The process provides only what you need to participate. Never direction or choices for the sufficiency of the Continuum knows your name for only one end.

The only thing that is constant is the Continuum. The process of the Continuum is always. What that process is can never be the same. The flux of life ripples into infinite shapes for endless purpose with dimensions only the human mind limits. There is no way to impede it yet so many try. In their inability to accept the ever changing nature of the Continuum life becomes combative rather than compassionaire, difficult rather than harmonious, scarce rather than bountiful. The nature of the Contuuum will never change because of the choices that mankind makes in walking their spiritual pathway. The Continuum will never be stopped, altered , or accelerated by any individual. For an individual to attempt to do so merely adds a needed experience and lesson learned onto their ultimate goal of individual spiritual perfection. Live life for it lives for you!

Salvatore N. Balletto
Returned to me by Tao Chin Sai E'
my spiritual guide May/June 1990

AWARENESS

Awareness without giving
    is like the Ocean without tide
Giving without receiving
    is like the tide without Sound
For Awareness
    Giving
        Receiving
are as one

Awareness without love
    is like a bud that never blooms
Love without compassion
    is like a flower without seeds
For Awareness
    Love
        Compassion
are as one

Awareness without Understanding
    is like life without Soul
Understanding without forgiving
    is like Soul without Spirit
For Awareness
    Understanding
        Forgiving
are as one

Awareness without Harmony
 is like touch without feeling
Harmony without Stillness
 is like feeling without emotion
For Awareness
 Harmony
 Stillness
are as one

Life without Awareness
 is like walking without Knowledge
Awareness without Spirit
 is like Knowledge without Discovery
For Life
 Awareness
 Spirit
are as one

QUESTIONS

§

There are only three important questions.

Know their answers.

Who am I?

§

This is under your control and is never free. Remember, whatever you are will always be. Your material things are only results you see.

Your choices, your values, your actions are the essence of the weave.

Will, effort, persistence are payment please...

Will you like the footprints that you leave?

Why am I here?

§

Truth, Compassion, Judgment, Freedom are some examples for you but perhaps not me. Have you taken the time to listen to the sea?

Love, Love yourself, Love one another, Love Life... this one is for you and me.

The answer is within the expression of your uniqueness. Take the time to be still then ask listen and love all of thee.

Where am I going?

§

Seeing your pathway and walking that pathway are not the same. Are you aware but still not there? There is no one else to blame.

Life is not a game.

Your life is Your Choices reflected by Your Values put into Your Action to create Your Karma.

The results shall eternally be your name.

Do not be concerned with time...it only has value when you are not aware of it.

Life's significance does not know time.

Do not be concerned with another's pathway... it is not your own. Others may cast a light but you must have the courage to walk yours alone.

Life's most significant pathways only have one set of footprints.

Do not be concerned with power. It will never leave you alone!

Life's most significant control is by you, for you, alone.

Do not covet material things... they add nothing to your real value.

Life's most significant values will eternally be your own.

Do not be concerned with judgment... it will leave you alone.

Life's most significant conclusions are by you, for you, alone.

Life's Lessons Learned

Walk Softly, Your Steps are Known

Speak Softly, Your Words are Heard

Touch Softly, Your Hands are Loved

<u>*Because*</u>

§

Strength Needs no Force

Truth Needs no Words

Love Needs no Touch

How small

a grain of time

a wisp of selfishness

and our world

How large

a grain of awareness

a wisp of giving

and our love

Be Quiet and know yourself

Find Peace within and

Touch All with Harmony

Solar Eclipse. Photograph by Rev. Dr. Eugene C. Larr

A Spiritual Definition of Man

Love is when we experience together
                    with our lives and our souls

On the Truth:

"Why do you search the world to know? Do not move outward in but inward out. The sound of your silence holds all the answers. The bullseye of knowing is as large as yourself. The arrow moves from your heart in the light of the truth never to know doubt again".

Tao Chin 7/30/92

"The sound of the truth is heard in silence.
The light of the truth is not counted in numbers.
The way of the truth creates no pathway.

The sound of the truth has no echo.
The light of the truth casts no shadow.
The way of the truth creates no pathway."

Light Hawk 9/16/92

"Do not hold the cactus with your hand. If it's the center you seek let the knife of Knowing be your plan."

Light Hawk 7/31/92

Success results from

daily expression

of yourself with

persistence of sharing

and a love of life

Perfection

*All things must come to perfection through their own
efforts through their own pathway
in their own time*

Time

§

*You cannot live tomorrow today. Nor should you let
yesterday's shadow darken today. Let today be a joy
unto itself! Be totally where you are so that you can be
totally all that you are. Remember...*

*"You cannot pry open a flower bud
it must open itself to perfection"*

Pathway

§

*Your pathway to perfection has only one set of footprints.
Do not listen for the echo of another. Your experience of
perfection may be much shorter than your pathway. Enjoy
the process. Remember...*

*Your uniqueness will cast the light
but you must have the courage
to follow the way*

Effort

§

Perfection given is not perfect at all. Experience adds to your knowledge. Knowledge does not add to your experience. The pathways of life must be walked for you to reach your goal. Remember…

*The flower once in bloom
cannot be forced to do so again
Your efforts
must be in tune with your pathway
then in time
you will bloom again and again!*

Man the Student 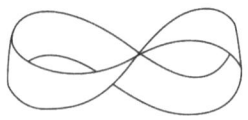 *Nature the Teacher*

The Sun offers its energy

Do you not accept its warmth?

The Rain embraces the living

Do you not let it hold you?

The Wind whispers to the leaves

Do you not hear their love song?

The Ocean caresses the shore

Do you not understand its lessons?

*To love Nature
is to hear
to understand
to heed her*

*Are you
truly aware?*

COURAGE

I am not going to emphasize the kind of courage we see on television or the movies or perhaps witness in a rare circumstance in life-threatening situations. But, rather, I am going to concentrate on the type of courage it takes to live our everyday lives while remaining on the pathway of self-truth.

The concept of courage is closely related to Self-Truth. However knowing your truth and following that self-truth are two different things. The element that connects them is courage.

Courage is the ACTION of self-realization through the light of self-truth.

That is the kind of courage I want to discuss in this article. Okay, so how do we get courageous? I think for most of us this is a very slow process. First we must decide that remaining faithful to our self-truth is the best way to advance ourselves spiritually and physically. Courage, like so many other aspects of life, starts within us. Courage is the result of deep self-understanding, deep self-acceptance and a deep dedication to self-truth. The best way to develop those characteristics is through listening to the sound of your silence every day. Yes, it all goes back to stillness meditation, again and again!

Let's get real practical here and look at a very important aspect of life and see how courage relates to it. Love is something that all of us are here to experience in its many different manifestations. One of the best descriptions of love that I have heard came from a movie entitled, "Love Story" (starring Ali McGraw and Ryan O'Neil). It was, "Being in love means never having to say you are sorry."

My definition of love is a sharing of our highest values, our lives, across the infinite dimension of time for the highest purpose; the fulfillment of life.

Loving someone takes courage. You have to treat that other person as you would treat yourself. That means you will indeed never have to say you are sorry. That takes courage. You have to care for that person when they may not be able to care for themselves. That takes courage. You have to let that person be who only they can be, while sharing your lives together at every level. That takes courage. Your love will only endure if you surrender to that person and they surrender to you. That takes courage.

So where is love? Your first step to finding love is to make the choice of love. This relates very strongly, of course, to your commitment to self-truth. We are all here for the experience of love in one or more of its dimensions. Your next step is to learn to love yourself completely. Guess what that relates to? Self-understanding and self-acceptance. Finally you must learn to see the beauty in all of life. Then when you have experienced those things you will know your heart and have the COURAGE to follow it.

Sometimes, do you think we will lose courage? Well, I think that most of us know the answer to that question. Of course, we can lose courage simply because our foundation for the manifestation of courage is not perfect. Our self-understanding, self-acceptance, and dedication to self-truth are not going to be perfect. It is important, it is really important, to realize that when we do lose courage, when we waiver in the face of fear, we must be kind to ourselves. Why? Because kindness to ourselves is the beginning of the process of growing more courageous.

Fear, false energy appearing real, fear is always going to plague us in one of its many manifestations. This is where if I was going to use an analogy I would compare this to a weight lifter trying to lift a weight that is beyond his capabilities. Does the weight lifter give up because he cannot lift that weight? Not if he is going to get stronger. Like that weight lifter, we could be training our minds to be more courageous. We do this by taking the time each day to improve our self- understanding, self-acceptance, and knowledge of self-truth through stillness meditation. If we take the time for ourselves, each day, to build our mental muscles we can build our potential. Then, when fear tests our courage, we will be able to lift more and more.

But those times will come when we will lose courage. We are all human beings. When fear confronts us with a test that is beyond our current capabilities, it is important then to be kind to ourselves. Realize that kindness to yourself opens the door to greater courage. Only by being kind to yourself when you lose courage will you find yourself back on the road to greater courage.

Life takes a great deal of courage for us to manifest to our full potential, spiritually and physically; to manifest what only we can be. If you are going to be able to lift those weights, you are going to have to be working out every day. You must be listening to the sound of your silence every day. You must take the time each day to nurture yourself, to understand yourself, accept yourself, and rededicate yourself to self- truth. No one can do this for you. No one.

You are going to be amazed at the person that emerges from this process. It is going to be a person that judges far less and in this non-judgement finds greater peace of mind. Someone that in his greater self-acceptance finds much greater acceptance of different peoples and different lifestyles. It is going to be a person with much greater self-understanding and in this understanding find the ability to not only forgive but to forget. It will be a person of much greater awareness and in this greater awareness you will be bringing into your life the changes and type of people that you want. You will be in the river of life. You will be in the flow of change. But the quiet places, the rapids, the waterfalls, will be occurring in your time and on your time. Less and less will things be happening to you. More and more will you be happening to things.

Finally, another amazing thing that is going to happen in this process is that, as you grow more and more courageous, it will seem that you need less and less courage. You see, Fear will have less and less opportunity in your life!

To reach this level is indeed going to take years of dedicated work. I am not underestimating this. But it is there for all of us. Each of us can build the kind of courage that leaves very little room for fear. I can only urge you to participate in this process because it will really be the dawning of a better life.

A life filled with much greater rewards, both physically and spiritually.

Remember, the essence of poverty is one without courage to make his dreams be. Security captivates, fear destroys, courage liberates! Your dreams light the pathway but you must have the courage to be thee. Your time, your energy, your imagination, are the fuel that they need. The expectations are high; it is your spirit they heed. The limits that exist are of you, by you, for you, can you not see? Your time first to be still then to understand and let yourself be free.

Salvatore Balletto

"Those with Awareness always sense what Time it is.

There is a Time to know.
  There is a Time not to know.
    There is a Time to Share.
      There is a Time not to Share.
        There is a Time to support Change.
          There is a Time to let Change be with others.
            There is always Time for Love.
              Only those who nurture Love within will know its blessings
                There is never Time for hatred.
                  For without Love you will only hurt yourself.

Those with Awareness always sense what Time it is."

Given to me by Tao Chin Lao Sai E' on 10/15/2017

Your dreams are your future and what you could be. Remember, your expectations–not mine, not theirs. Are you going to like the image you see?

Salvatore Balletto

"A fragrance once sensed is always remembered."

"Sit still and then with silent mind ask."

"Do not be Concerned with time... it was invented by Man."

"Are you truly who you think you are?"

Walk Softly, Strength Needs no Force

Speak Softly, Truth needs no Words

Touch Softly, Love Needs no Touch

<u>Because</u>

§

Your Steps are Known

Your Words are Heard

Your Hands are Loved

THE BUILDING BLOCKS OF LIFE

A Definition of Life

The essence of the weave. This is our goal. To touch the primary indivisible aspects of the physical plane. The keys to the doors that unlock the answers to the three important questions in life. Who am I? Why am I here? Where am I going? They are not the answers but rather a way for us to create, understand, and change the answers to those questions.

Unavoidable and irreducible: this is the acid test. Unavoidable but under our control. Irreducible. From them spring many important aspects of life, below them only fragments of the living experience.

The Building Blocks of Life are Volition, Change, Karma, and Love.

Volition simply stated is our ability to exercise our will and hence make choices in every aspect of our lives. This is our unique opportunity as human beings. Lower forms of existence follow instinctive patterns of behavior in a large part of their lives. It's the human mode of existence and many of us try to avoid it! We try to get others to make choices for us or just do not make any choices at all. But when we fail to make a decision that, in itself, is a decision. When we allow, demand, or legislate others to make decisions for us that, in itself, is a decision. Unavoidable. Our control is obvious. That this process can be positive is our choice.

Change is the only constant in the universe. Change is part of life; life is part of change. To direct it requires your mental control. The things that you do not want in your life will soon find the door marked "Exit" when you exercise your volition, recognize the nature of the ever changing process, and use the power of your mind to direct the symphony of living.

Our Third Building Block of Life, Karma, is simple causation. Karma is cause and effect. Karma is the process by which the message we send out in our lives through the exercise of our own volition, is the message we will in turn receive through the process of change. It is important to realize that this process may not manifest exactly in the way we anticipate, nor may be as quick as you desire, but it does work and it is unavoidable.

The final Building Block of Life is Love. To see its unavoidability is to discover its many dimensions. Lovers, wives, husbands, friends, relatives, pets, ourselves, it seems to never end. To be without some form of love in your life is to shrivel up and just go away.

To see its irreducibility is to know that love is more than an emotion. We can do without hate, grief, or sadness in our lives, but we cannot do without love. Love is a confirmation of life. A reward for the living. A way of saying I am (volition), I have (change), I will (karma). Love is the spirit of the Body of Life.

There are many "important" aspects of life which are not Building Blocks of Life. This is justly so. The Building Blocks of Life represent a definition of life and as such should be common to all human beings. What is "important" to one may not be "important" to another; but this should not alter the primary significance of the Building Blocks of Life in each person's experience if indeed, they represent a definition of life.

Some examples of these other "important" aspects of life are:

Death, which is unavoidable but not irreducible. It is part of the Building Block of Change. This reflects the relative unimportance of death in our life experience. We all have done it many times and will do it many more times again.

Values which is simply stated what we choose to gain and/or keep. Values determine our emotional make-up and hence, indeed, are "important" as well as unavoidable, but they are not irreducible. Values stem from the Building Block of Volition.

The Building Blocks of Life are a way of illustrating your utter control over your development. You need not be very intelligent, talented, or beautiful to have a life of harmony, wellness, and prosperity. You "only" need be in control of your tool for participating in life through the human mode of existence: your mind.

Salvatore Balletto

AGING

The essence of old is in your mind.
Create, accept, understand the lessons of life.

It is not necessary to be blind.

The essence of old is in your mind.
Start today! Enjoy each part of your life.

Is it not necessary to be this kind?

The essence of old is in your mind.
When your body needs - listen, rest, heal.

It is necessary each day for all mankind.

The essence of old is in your mind.
When your spirit speaks and you know then...

Young is yours for all time.

"Fear Not, Want Not"

Tao Chin
April 10, 1991

Ask and you shall receive

    Know and you shall achieve.

The pinnacle is oh so far yet so near. The pathway to the top can never be without experience, triumph, and defeat.

Fear is the hollow essence of defeat.

    Knowing is the Light Without Shadow on your pathway to achievement.

                                    Tao Chin Lao Sai E
                                           10/22/98

THE HUMAN MODE OF EXISTENCE

'Each creature has its place...Mankind will one day find his.'

As human beings one of the most fundamental and unique choices we make in our lives is how and to what degree we will interact with our environment at the conceptual level of consciousness, as well as how and to what degree this will promote life. In other words, how human we are going to be. In other words, how much we are going to live as opposed to just surviving.

The Human Mode of Existence is my way of describing mankind's place in the universe. The use of our mind's conceptual level consciousness to interact with the total environment in a way that promotes life is the pathway of mankind that leads to living, not just survival.

It is a place only we can occupy. A place of life for the living of living for the promotion of life. A place of knowing and using that knowing to cast a light without shadow.

Only mankind has the power to choose life or death. The responsibility to know the consequences of his activities. The ability to see what is and know what can be. The will to change conditions of life. The mind to bring the joy of living to the universe.

'Within the mind is the universe, or is the universe the mind?'

Within each of our minds resides a limitless capacity that becomes indistinguishable from the infinite embrace of the universe. We have the power and choice to develop this capacity or abuse it, exercise it or neglect it, but we will never be able to avoid the consequences of these fundamental choices. They will be the difference between life or death, living or just survival, achievement or mediocrity.

As each of us moves toward our own perfection through our own unique pathway, the universe and our minds will stretch toward unity. This unity will place us in an instinctive harmony with all of life.

This is the unique challenge that life places before Mankind's Pathway. It is a challenge that resonates within your hands now. Holding it with your mind you cannot but know it. Walk it with your life and you will know the only meaning of the words peace, harmony, and prosperity.

Salvatore Balletto

LOVE

*Two minds can never be as one
But they can touch, softly*

*Two hearts can never be as one,
But they can love, completely*

*Two people can never be as one,
But they can walk, side by side*

"The changes of your life are like a river. There are quiet places, rapids, and waterfalls. On your way to merging with the big water realize that each place has its own conditions and requirements. Understand that being in the river means accepting these changes. Being in control means letting these changes occur in your time and on your time."

Light Hawk 9/14/92

Because the eagle flies it must land. Because the eagle lands it can fly. Immerse yourself in life. In the seed of failure lies success. In the experience of success fear was overcome."

Light Hawk 5/1/92

*"Love is when two people
walk the same pathway
without following
in each other's footprints."*

Light Hawk

LOVE

Love has many dimensions: psychological, physical, and most importantly spiritual. What distinguishes love from other emotions is its spiritual necessity. That is what makes Love a Building Block of Life. We can do without hate, anxiety, greed, fear and many other emotions but we cannot survive, literally survive, without some form of love in our lives.

Love has many manifestations: friends, family, pets, spouses, children, self, to mention just a few. The facets and diversity of love make it both interesting and difficult to discuss in a comprehensive way.

First, looking at love from a "strictly" psychological point of view, it is an emotion. What causes emotions? Is it possible to understand and control our emotions?

Emotions are a value response. A value is what we seek to gain or keep. Values can be physical or non-physical. For example, they can represent concepts like honesty, ambition, or integrity. On a more physical level they can be a Mercedes Benz or a diamond ring. We acquire our values sometimes unconsciously, sometimes consciously. Most people do not think about, or select, their values. Most people merely adopt the value system they have been taught by their parents or teachers or accept the values of their peers or society as a whole. Because of this the values can be inconsistent with each other and can actually be detrimental to the promotion of life or happiness.

Emotions are a value response. For example, if we have accepted honesty as a value and observe someone who in his actions is dishonest and greedy, "we do not like that person."

However, values can be selected consciously and integrated into your subconscious mind. Selecting values and integrating them into your mind is an act of volition; another Building Block of Life.

This process is unique to Mankind. This is exclusively a human experience. It is part of what I call the human mode of existence. Clearly animals have emotions but they are based on values which are instinctive. They acquire this information before incarnating.

They cannot select their values much less choose values that are inimical to their lives.

Once these values do become fully integrated, your emotions relevant to these values will be automatic and instantaneous. This quite simply means that if you are willing to put forth the mental effort and energy to select and integrate your values you can have control over your value responses, that is, your emotions.

The degree to which this is accomplished will determine the degree of your control. The degree to which these values are consistent with each other and beneficial to life, the greater will be your sense of inner peace.

The degree to which people like each other is the degree to which they share their values. Psychologically, love in some form is a very high degree of value agreement between two people.

Now, this explains love as an emotion. This does not explain the essential nature of love in some form in our lives. This is an adequate description for all emotions except love.

It is not a complete definition of love because it does not touch upon the spiritual necessity of love.

What is the complete understanding of love? When you give love and receive love you are saying, I am, you are; I am fit for life, you are fit for life; I celebrate who I am within the person you are and you celebrate the person you are within the person I am. Together we can experience life with our love, without judgment, demands or control. This kind of reward from the living to the living is the spiritual fuel that we all must have to keep the flame of life burning. This kind of spiritual sharing adds meaning to the pursuit of all our other values.

Love casts a light without shadow on our pathway of life. This is why love is a spiritual necessity.

This kind of loving experience does not have to be sexual. It can be between friends or relatives. This level of love does have to be between two human beings because of the conceptual level of awareness required.

Most importantly, loving who you are metaphysically or spiritually is a prerequisite to this kind of love. Obviously you cannot celebrate who you are within another person until you have come to understand and love yourself spiritually.

Now for the physical element of love. When the physical or sexual element is present we call this romantic love. Romantic love, for many of us, is the most sought after and the most elusive form of love. Why is that? First of all, romantic love requires that you have integrated into your mind a value system that is very consistent and beneficial to life. Secondly, romantic love requires that you have truly come to a complete understanding, acceptance, and love of who you are physically, as well as metaphysically. The only way I know of to accomplish that (there may be other ways but I do not know of them) is by listening to the sound of your silence every day.

Yes, I am talking about meditation practices. Daily stillness meditation will deepen your understanding of yourself and the world we live in. That is the beginning of celebrating life through the expression of who you are. That kind of human action is the foundation of love.

Many of us, in our frustration, try to substitute a sexual relationship for romantic love. Doesn't work out that well, does it? There is no short cut to this supreme reward life has to offer. You have to earn it. One of my spirit guides (his name is Light Hawk) describes romantic love as when two people walk the same pathway without following in each other's footprints.

You earn it by being very positive with yourself and your partner; being very aware of who they are within you and who you are within them; and by walking a pathway of harmony with all living things.

Again, the only way I know of to get into that space is through your ever growing awareness.

Salvatore Balletto

PERFECTION, PEACE AND PROSPERITY

The world is filled with Perfection camouflaged by imperfection.

> *Those who profess disdain of error yet find its company only halter their minds.*
>
> *Do not judge others; judge only yourself only when absolutely necessary and only with the highest degree of kindness.*
>
> *Perfection walks in many pathways, in many forms, toward one goal: the fulfillment of life through self-understanding, self-acceptance, and self-realization.*

The World is filled with conflict submerged in the hunger for Peace.

> *Seeking control outside of you always means surrender of your peace of mind.*
>
> *Do not seek to control others. The greatest achievements lie within your mind. Learn to control and release its energy and your name will echo throughout time.*
>
> *Peace sleeps within each of us to be awakened with self understanding developed through self-acceptance and finally satisfied through self-realization. When you have achieved this self-esteem, it will manifest for all mankind.*

The world is filled with want while standing knee deep in prosperity.

> *Material success can leave you with hollow comfort.*
>
> *Know the difference between want and need. Your material needs seek you. Your material wants lead you. Know the difference between survival and living. Survival is life without purpose. Living is purpose within life.*

Prosperity is success in living. Prosperity walks a pathway of peace in the light of perfection seeing only you.

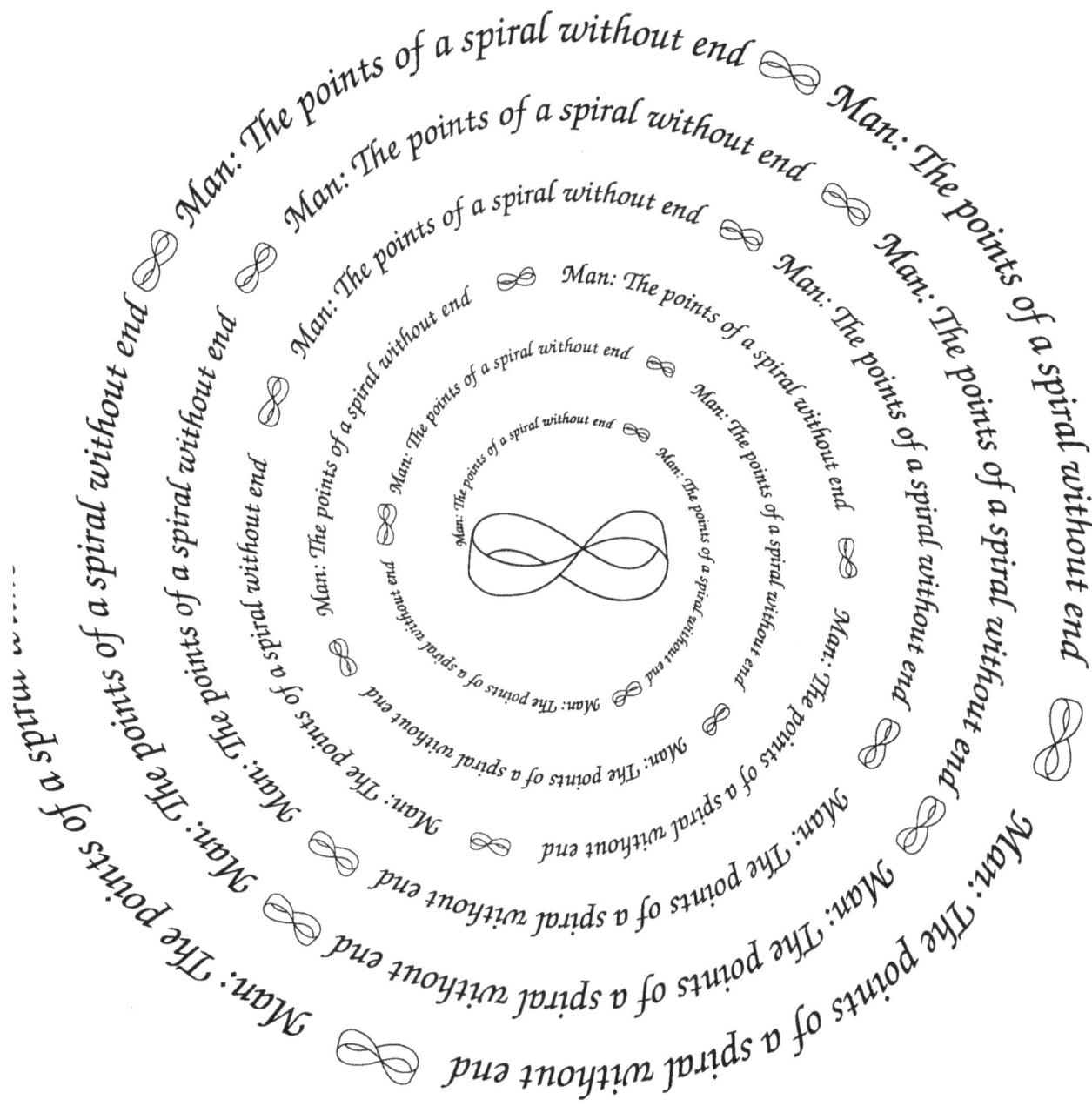

A Spiritual Definition of Man

Live each day in harmony with nature's laughter

Laugh each day to celebrate life's renewal of love

Love each day so that you may fulfill yourself through sharing

Share each day for the reward of sharing is success!

March, 1991

*"How old
are you?
Ask a star
and ponder."*

*"Through the thunder
of the mind
nothing
can be heard."*

*"Listen
to the symphony,
it is all around
you, now!"*

*"Two minds can
never be as one,
but they can
touch, softly."*

I Asked Spirit

I asked Spirit to help me find love
    Spirit said
Need love
Give love
and you shall receive love

I asked Spirit to help me find purpose
    Spirit said
You are the purpose

I asked Spirit to help me find truth
    Spirit said
Truth is all around you
You need only be aware and accept it

    Then Spirit said
You have found me only because you have
searched with stillness within yourself
Continue that search long enough and all
    questions will cease

Walk with experience out of yesterday

into today toward tomorrow with

knowledge of your pathway

April 24, 1991

Walk life's pathway with Awareness

Light life's pathway with truth

Experience life's pathway with Love

Tao Chin in Dark Circle
January 29, 1991

THE HARMONIOUS LIFE

The harmonious life, what does that really mean and can I accomplish it? The harmonious life is about balancing the physical needs of our existence with the metaphysical needs of our happiness. The harmonious life is about balancing our wants with our needs. Perhaps most importantly, the harmonious life is about understanding the difference between the meaning of life and the purpose of life, AND LIVING ACCORDINGLY.

What is the source, the foundation, of this kind of life and how can we build and preserve that foundation? Certainly, we live in a very disharmonious world. There is constant war, famine, and discord. We have to be able to, at least to some degree, insulate ourselves from all this chaos. Being untouchable? How do we do that? Drink the right cool aid?

It becomes clear that no one on the physical plane will reach total harmony. Those individuals who have reached total harmony no longer need to be here. They are called avatars.

In fact, it becomes clear that the discord we are immersed in is part of the reason why we are here. It is part of the purpose of life. We would not be able to progress to our own individual spiritual perfection without the constant challenges that the physical world throws at us. But, and this is an important but, although we are immersed in the river of change, challenges, and discord, the rapids, the waterfalls, and the quiet moments can be made to occur in our time and on our time. That is what a harmonious life is about: Not quite untouchable, but in control of our lives by dealing from a deck stacked in our favor, and dealing with reality in a way that is inward out, not outward in. This is an indication of how we go about creating this lifestyle.

Well, so how do we go about building this type of harmony? First of all, by building a harmonious space within ourselves, with ourselves, and for ourselves through stillness meditation. This will take a daily commitment to build and sustain your inner peace. When you enter and develop this kind of space you will diminish your desires for excesses in our material existence.

Secondly, it is NOT by trying to control people and things outside of you. The more you attach and attempt to control events and people around you, the more disharmony you will bring into your life.

So, yes, you need the cooperation and assistance of others around you to live life. But the harmonious way to accomplish that is by mutual consent for mutual benefit. As your stillness practices become more regular and advanced, your desire for this kind of control will dissolve away.

Thirdly, the final building block of harmony is LOVE. The practice of sharing your inner peace that you have worked so hard to develop with those around you will bring a confirmation of life that makes it all worthwhile.

So, what are the hallmarks of a harmonious life? How will you know you have achieved this status? Well, there are some signposts. Some of them are illustrated in a poem by Oriah Mountain Dreamer called, "The Invitation" that I have modified to some degree for this essay. They go like this:

If you will risk looking like a fool for your love, for your spirit, for the adventure of being alive.

If life's betrayals have made you wiser and more compassionate, instead of becoming old and closed from fear of further pain.

If you can be joyful. If you can celebrate and let the ecstasy fill you to the tips of your fingers and toes without cautioning yourself to be careful, to be realistic, and to remember the limitations of being human.

If you can disappoint another to be true to who you are. If you can bear the accusation of betrayal and not betray your own spirit. If you can be faithless and therefore trustworthy.

If each day you can see beauty in life, even when it is not obvious, and if you can motivate your actions from its presence.

If you can live with failure and STILL stand at the edge of the lake and shout to the silver of the full moon "YES!" in full knowledge that all your failures are only temporary; in full knowledge that each success and each failure are additional steps forward in your progress to your own personal perfection.

If you can get up after the night of grief and despair, weary and bruised to the bone, and do what needs to be done to sustain your spirit and soul.

If you know what sustains you from the inside when all else falls away and so can stand in the center of the fire with your values and not shrink back when life rages ferociously.

If you can be alone with yourself and truly like the company you keep, in those moments of listening to the sound of your silence.

These characteristics and actions would certainly be testimony to your harmonious space.

So, back to the beginning, now that we are at the end. What is the difference between the meaning of life and the purpose of life?

I am tempted to let you discover the answer to that question when you reach your harmonious space. For your answer may be a little different from mine. My answer is: The purpose of life is to provide you with the "vehicle" to reach your own spiritual perfection. To provide you with the means to have experiences, some of which we dread, some of which we love, some of which we try to avoid, and all of which give you the ability to advance. We choose some of these opportunities while still on spirit side before incarnating.

The meaning of life, of course, is the experience of love in its many facets and expressions. By experiencing love in different ways, at different times in your development, your perfection is distilled. Without these experiences you would not reach perfection.

By building a Harmonious Life you not only increase the joy of living but accelerate your progress to perfection so that you too will not have to come back here again. Trust me, spirit side is a lot nicer than this side. The simple practice of stillness meditation can bring it to you, lay it all at your feet for the taking!

Salvatore Balletto

A Pathway to Love Through Self-Realization

I can only be what I am.

I can only walk my pathway following the light of truth for that is all I can see.

If in that walking we can hold hands, that will only bring greater joy to you and me.

June 10, 1991

*You can hold with your words as well as
 your hands*

*You can see with your mind as well as
 your eyes*

*You can listen with your heart as well as
 your ears*

*You can love with your spirit as well as
 your body*

*Learn from Yesterday
 Love Today*

Be Aware of Tomorrow

"The Pathway of greatest potential holds only one set of footprints"

Light Hawk
April 10, 1991

Love

Love is a sharing of our highest value - our lives - across the infinite dimension of time for the greatest purpose; the fulfillment of life.

Where is Love?

Your first step to finding love is to make the choice of love

Your next step is to learn to love yourself completely

Finally learn to see the beauty in all of life

Then when you have experienced these things you will know your heart....

Follow it!

The Rewards of Love

The knowing without speaking
The sharing without asking
The commitment without sacrifice

Originally Received: October 31, 1998 by Salvatore Balletto from Lord of Light

Transcribed on: January 23, 2017

Asked Lord of Light what spirit side is like.

"Truly a place of ultimate self control. Here your associations are of your choice without interference. Your control over your space and your development is truly without hindrance. A place in which your stretch to infinity is limitless. Only here can you know it all and have it all. Life without the physical needs will for you be one of the crowning achievements of your perfection."

Lord of Light
10/31/98

Remark: Got additional information that development on spirit side is very possible and usually after perfection is reached.

YOUR DREAMS

Your Time, Your Imagination, Your Energy is the fuel they need. The expectations are high. Remember, it is your spirit they heed.

Your time for recognition. Your dreams are you and what your future could be. Remember; your expectations not mine or theirs, do you like the image you see?

Your Imagination, first to be still, then to understand and let yourself be free. Remember; the limits that exist are of you, by you, for you, can you not see?

Your Energy. The essence of poverty is one without desire to make his dreams be! Security captivates. Dreams liberate. Do you not agree? Your Dreams light the pathway but you must have the courage to be thee.

Fear knocked at the door, Truth answered, no one was there.

Awareness casts the light from within that illuminates our pathway without shadow

Compassion conveys understanding of the needs of others without fear

Truth is the catalyst for self-realization without disharmony

Love is the life process in its full expression wrapped with compassion, realized through truth, and focused with awareness.

"If you are walking in the darkness of your own shadow you must be moving in the wrong direction. Why walk in darkness when light without shadow can be your way. Aware and Awake you will move from light to light without the shadow of fear knowing your name."

*Light Hawk
June 11, 1992*

Listen to the symphony;
it is all around you, now

Listen to the Symphony, can you Hear life breathing? Do you See the color of life? Do you Feel life's heartbeat against your outstretched hand, now?!

Being in touch with life means being in touch with yourself. Being in touch with yourself means being in touch with life. You can escape life through self denial, or celebrate it through self realization.

Listen to the symphony;
it is all around you, now

Life lives for you but you must live for life if you are to know its exquisite subtle joys, feel its exhilarating triumphs, overcome its constant challenges, move like a well placed arrow straight to the bulls eye of knowing.

Can you hold back your energy from true love? Then why do you wiggle your toes in life's pool of dreams, challenges, questions and answers, triumphs and defeats? Life draws you toward it with experiences that need your name.

Listen to the symphony;
it is all around you, now

Fear not failure for in your courage lies the seed of success, in your energy the Spring of prosperity, in your knowing the full Summer of satisfaction. Fear not the Winters of life for then your pathway will melt all obstacles. The full symphony of life is then the rhythm of your life force, never to know limits again.

Listen to the Symphony. It is the song of your life, all around you, now!

"The gathering of eagles always brings the whispering of wings. Listen to your wings not the many directions of the wind. Look through your eyes not through the light of another. Then you will fly without shadow, see without light, and soar without wind."

Light Hawk
February 20, 1992

THE TRUTH

Jesus was asked many times, "who or what is God?" He replied "God is spirit. Thee who would believe in him would believe in spirit and the TRUTH."

What is the truth? How do you think Jesus would have answered that question?

Spirit has given me principal characteristics of the truth.

They are: "The SOUND of the truth is heard in silence. The VALIDITY of the truth is not counted in numbers. The WAY of the truth creates no pathway. The LIGHT of the truth casts no shadow." These principles will form the outline for this essay.

"The Sound of the Truth is Heard in Silence"

Another way of saying this that I have often used is: Listen to the sound of your silence, all of the answers are there. You see, no one can give you the truth. You must experience the truth before you will understand, accept, and make it a part of your life. This book is a reflection of my learning, NOT YOURS. It is a reflection of my progress, NOT YOURS. It is a reflection of my experiences, NOT YOURS. Like any reflection it is something outside of you. Something you may see, hear, or touch, but it is not part of you. It will be your choices and your actions that change this reflection of my learning into a light that emits from within you.

If we listen to that inner voice, that inner voice that really has no sound but is rather a sense of what is right for us, we would rarely be off the pathway of self-truth.

Too many of us, though, want to move outward in, not inward out. We want to have all the material things that prosperity signifies before we ourselves emit the light of self-realization.

We want to have the outward rewards that happiness signifies before we ourselves emit the light of self-understanding and self-acceptance.

We want to have all the rewards that love from another reflects before we ourselves emit the light of self-love.

The actions necessary, and sufficient to create and sustain the truth, are primarily within ourselves. It deals with our own self-development. It is far more accurate to describe this process as creating the truth, not discovering the truth, because for each of you this process and its results are going to be unique.

The outward world is filled with the distraction of others walking their pathways, not your pathway, regardless of what they may say. Tuning into this process of knowing is not easy because we have been encouraged to disregard it, educated to know better, and sometimes ridiculed or punished if we acknowledge or follow it. Learning to be still and aware of who we are, why we are here, and where we are going, is a lifetimes endeavor. It never ceases but its rewards are continuous and cumulative. There is NOTHING more important than this search and development of self-truth.

"The Validity of the Truth is not Counted in Numbers"

This may seem a little strange. After all, do we not vote on many important issues so that the majority desire is acknowledged and followed? Will the opinion, decision or demands of others leave you off balance? Will you be standing in the light of self-truth when the shadow of others walking their pathways reaches you?

Be in a place, that special place of knowing without asking, understanding without verification, of action without doubt, that reflects your standing in the light of self-truth. Remember, the truth starts and ends with you. Realize that your truth is uniquely yours and follow its light to self-realization. Whenever it becomes necessary because of convention, tradition, or law to ask permission of others to proceed keep that process in its proper perspective.

"The Way of the Truth Creates no Pathway"

I think at this point you may have an inkling of why that is so. There is no magic bromide that will take us straight to Utopia. No Excalibur that, drawn and wielded, will slay all our enemies. The truth should not, actually cannot, be used to control or manipulate other people. When you encounter someone professing to know "the truth" and using that power to exercise control over others, know that their shadow is cast from untruth.

Finally we have .....

"The Light of the Truth Casts No Shadow"

The truth is a light, a light without shadow that illuminates for each of us our unique passage toward perfection. Inward out, not outward in. The bull's-eye of knowing is as large as yourself; as large as your acceptance of yourself, your understanding of yourself, your courage to remain faithful to yourself. How can you miss it if you touch, hear, experience the sound of your silence every day? The arrow will move from your heart, in the Light of the Truth, never to know doubt again. As you take the time each day to develop your awareness, this last sentence will become a constant experience in your life. The truth will become the catalyst in your life for self-realization without disharmony. Fear may knock on your door. It does for all of us. But when you answer, emitting the Light of Self-Truth, no one will be there!

On the other hand, if you are walking in the darkness of your own shadow, you must be moving in the wrong direction. Why walk in darkness when light without shadow can be your way? Aware and Awake you will move from light to light without the shadow of fear knowing your name. Through the opening of your eyes will you see without light. Through the discovery of your voice will you speak without echo. Through the opening of your ears WILL YOU HEAR ONLY THE TRUTH!

My highest Blessing,

Salvatore N. Balletto

On Wisdom and The Wise

The wise man does not teach you his wisdom! For as each of you is an individual in spirit's embrace so will your understanding of spirit and the earth be unique. The wise man introduces you to yourself. Through the discovery of your voice will you speak with understanding. Through the opening of your ears will you hear while listening. Through the wings of this wisdom will you fly without fear.

www.ingramcontent.com/pod-product-compliance
Lightning Source LLC
Chambersburg PA
CBHW041529220426
43671CB00002B/29